One Woman's Struggle

Yahya Bekkaoui

One Woman's Struggle
Copyright © 2015 Yahya Bekkaoui

All rights reserved. No part of this book may be reproduced (except for inclusion in reviews), disseminated or utilized in any form or by any means, electronic or mechanical, including photocopying, recording, or in any information storage and retrieval system, or the Internet/World Wide Web without written permission from the author or publisher.

Book design by:
Arbor Books, Inc.
www.arborbooks.com

Printed in the United States of America

One Woman's Stuggle
Yahya Bekkaoui

1. Title   2. Author   3. Memoir

ISBN: 978-0-692-52446-6

LCCN: 2015914444

Table of Contents

CHAPTER 1	1953	1
CHAPTER 2	1969	6
CHAPTER 3	1971	12
CHAPTER 4	1972	19
CHAPTER 5	1974	25
CHAPTER 6	1976	30
CHAPTER 7	1977	35
CHAPTER 8	1977	43
CHAPTER 9	1992	49
CHAPTER 10	1998	54
CHAPTER 11	1999	58
CHAPTER 12	2003	63
CHAPTER 13	2004	67
CHAPTER 14	2005	71

Chapter 1

1953

Habiba was a beautiful girl both inside and out. On the day she was born, her parents laughed and smiled over her little locks of curly black hair; her dark, almond-shaped eyes; and her smooth brown skin. She cooed and blinked and looked around at this world she had been born into, all full of colors and lights and sound.

Morocco in the 1950s was in tumult: The sultan had been expelled from the country by the French governing party, and a revolution to get out from under foreign rule was underway. There were great disagreements, fighting in the streets even, but there was progress too—particularly in Casablanca, where Habiba's family lived. Casablanca was a truly contemporary city that followed the Western wave of modernism in its architecture and its arts. Known as a haven for writers, it attracted tourists from all over the world, so many that new hotels and restaurants seemed to be popping up every day. And so many people were moving into the city from the countryside, where they had lived for generations, that new residences were perpetually being built.

This progress was good for Habiba's family. Her father owned a sawmill that produced timber for construction companies; his business was quite successful, and it could be said their family was wealthy. In fact, his wood had been used in erecting the residences where he and his wife and new daughter lived, in a neighborhood of townhouse-style homes on a quiet city street. Their home rose three floors high; Habiba and her parents lived on the top floor, her aunt and uncle and their children on the second, and her mother's parents on the first. Like most other families in Morocco at the time, theirs was close knit and did not usually mind such close quarters. They loved spending time together and took care of one another no matter what.

However, Habiba didn't know about any of that yet. She was just a baby and then a child—her parents' only offspring, as a matter of fact, until she was four years old, when her brother, Hamid, was born. Habiba was so excited to have a baby brother and couldn't wait until he was old enough to be her playmate. Until then she helped her mother with taking care of him, even volunteering to feed him and change his diapers.

In this way Habiba and her brother became close. She loved him so much and showered him with affection every day, always kissing and hugging him and making up special games for him to play. She took him around the neighborhood, pushing him in his pram, and later, when he could walk, holding his hand so he wouldn't run off. She taught him not to go out in the streets, where the speeding cars and trucks could run him over, and introduced him to the nice man who owned the produce store down the street and the lady who sat outside her house with her cat all day. Habiba knew everyone around where she lived, and they were always so happy to see her.

"Here, Habiba, take whatever you like," the man at the fruit store would say to her, gesturing his hand across crates full of plums, oranges, bananas, apples, persimmons, and avocados.

"Thank you, Mr. Benali," she would say and choose one fruit for herself and one for Hamid.

Eventually Habiba lost her playmate when Hamid had to start going to school. Habiba remained at home with her mother, aunt, girl cousins, and grandmother, tending to the house and the younger children and cooking meals for her father and uncle when they came home from work. Sometimes she wished she could go to school too, to see what it was like and so she could spend more time with Hamid, whom she missed terribly. However, it was not allowed.

It was all right, though. Habiba was still a happy little girl and made the best of whatever situation life put her in. If Allah meant for her to stay at home and help her family, then that was for the best, and she tried to approach her many chores with as much of a positive attitude as possible. This was not difficult for her. Habiba had always been a happy child, and that wouldn't change no matter what.

The same could not be said, unfortunately, for Hamid. Ever since he was a baby, Habiba had noticed that he suffered from a sort of moodiness. One moment he would be smiling and cooing, playing with whatever small toy—a ball, a car, a small stuffed bear he seemed to favor—she was dangling in front of his face. Then the next it would be like a storm cloud had moved in over the top of his head. His smile would disappear, and he would begin to fuss, his little body fidgeting in his crib, his mouth opening wide to release a bloodcurdling scream.

Though the other children in the home were frightened of such cries and ran to get an adult whenever they heard one of Hamid's outbursts, Habiba felt nothing but love for her brother, and never more so than in those difficult moments. Though she was just a child herself, she would pick him up and hold him to her shoulder, bouncing on the balls of her feet as she paced back and forth across his nursery as she had seen her mother do. The movement seemed to lull him, and her quiet whispers—"Shhh, Hamid . . . Shhh . . ."—settled him down once again. Soon he would be asleep in her arms. Sometimes she put him back in his crib for his nap, but just as often she simply sat down on the floor and let him doze in her embrace.

As the two siblings grew together, Habiba's unerring spirit and optimistic outlook on life developed straight and true; never once did she feel anything other than a zest for life and a love for those who surrounded her and cared for her on a daily basis. The majority of her affection, of course, remained with Hamid, on whom she continued to dote. There was never a thought in her mind that did not involve him, never an activity she undertook that she didn't invite him to enjoy as well.

Hamid, on the other hand, grew in just the opposite way. Whereas his bad moods had been punctuated by fits of crying as an infant, as he became a boy they transformed into temper tantrums. If he didn't get what he wanted, if someone said something he didn't like, even if someone looked at him the wrong way, he would stamp his feet, cross his arms, and refuse to listen to whatever anyone had to say. No matter his parents' admonitions, no matter Habiba's promises of treats if he remained a good boy, it seemed he could not stop these negative spells from coming on. It was like they controlled him and not the other way around.

Habiba tried to understand why her brother was like this, but nothing in her could relate to his moods. Sure, she felt her share of negative emotions sometimes. She was disappointed when she looked forward to something and it did not happen; she became frustrated when she tried to master a task and could not do it right as quickly as she wanted. She was only human, after all. But she always knew that she could try again, that if she put her mind to it, she could obtain the outcome she desired. Hamid did not seem to have that reasoning, that means of seeing how the future might be. He simply wanted what he wanted right away, and when he didn't get it, his mood would take a turn for the worse.

Still, Habiba loved him. No matter what, they were brother and sister, and nothing—certainly not a bad mood once in a while—would ever change that.

Chapter 2

1969

At sixteen years old, Habiba was a stunning young woman, though she did not know this about herself. Her long, lustrous, and dark hair was simply a nuisance to wash, and she kept it pinned in a bun at the nape of her neck most of the time. Her dark eyes were sparkling with life, but all she knew was that they did not work as they should, and she'd had to start wearing glasses to read the many books she kept in a stack on the table beside her bed. Her tall, lithe body was not only attractive but strong, with muscles developed during her many years of cleaning and washing and lifting children—all the chores she continued without complaint under her mother's direction. Still, she kept her body covered up, dressing modestly at all times, unlike some of the women she saw on the streets these days wearing the Western styles—miniskirts, knee-high boots, and sweaters that showed off their curves. They looked good, she thought, even glamorous. But it simply was not the right look for her.

Instead Habiba moved throughout her days anonymously, neither looking to attract attention nor really receiving any. Those who saw her on a daily basis—Mr. Benali, who still owned the fruit store; the young man who delivered the bottles of milk to her house every morning; the son of the butcher at the shop where she bought lamb and chicken for her family to eat—of course noticed how pretty she was, but they also knew that Habiba was a private, humble person, and they respected her for that. She always came to partake of their services with a smile, with a kind word and inquiries about their families and friends. She knew the goings-on of everyone in her neighborhood but without being nosy or gossipy about it. She was simply interested in others. She was altruistic. And this came through in every word she said, every action that she did.

At home, Habiba approached her life with the same selflessness. Though she followed the same routine she had every day since she was a child—get out of bed at dawn, start the laundry, wash any dishes left in the sink, tend to her younger cousins, prepare the morning meal, and so on throughout the afternoon and evening as well—she did so with an air of optimism. She did not see her tasks as drudgery or as dreaded obligations but as opportunities to show her family over and over how much she loved them. In taking care of her aging parents and aunts and uncles as well as the younger children, she believed she was expressing to them how important they were to her. "Work is love made visible," as the poet Kahlil Gibran once said. She had read his book, *The Prophet*, and taken these words to heart.

The only thing that was missing from Habiba's good life was her brother, Hamid. While she still stayed and worked at home, he went to school, only now he was older and had been sent off to a boarding school, where he lived as well as studied. Habiba was happy for him; it was one of the best schools in the nation, and Hamid was fortunate to have been accepted there. But she missed him terribly. Where once they had been playmates as children, now they were the best of friends—confidantes, really, inseparable when Hamid was home on school breaks and vacations. But those short respites were so few and far between. For all intents and purposes, Hamid no longer lived with the family. He only came to visit.

Habiba found herself feeling lonely when her brother was not around to listen to her secrets, to play games with her, even to do something as simple as walk around the neighborhood with her. When he had to leave to go back to school, her cheeks were invariably stained with tears. She would stand outside their home, watching Hamid get into the car that would take him back to his boarding school while the driver stowed his suitcase in the trunk. As the car pulled away from the curb, Hamid would stick his head out the open back window and wave at Habiba until he was out of sight.

"Good-bye, brother," she would whisper, and she would stand alone at the top of the steps for some time, trying to compose herself. She couldn't go back inside and tend to the children in such a state.

On one such occasion, however, her silent reverie was interrupted.

"Such a beautiful young lady should not be so distraught," said a male voice, and Habiba quickly opened her eyes. Following the sound of it, she saw a young man standing outside the townhouse next door. He carried a brown cardboard box in his hands, and behind him was a truck with the logo of a moving company splashed across the side. Looking down at him from the top of the stairs, Habiba felt her face flush. He was handsome—rugged but well dressed, with short, wavy hair and a strong jaw. He looked young, maybe in his early twenties. "Oh, excuse me," she said, turning halfway away and bringing her hands up to dry her eyes. What a state for some strange man to see her in. She looked back at him over her shoulder. He still stood there looking at her with a bit of a smile on his face. "Sorry," she added, unsure of what to say to him.

"Please, don't apologize," he replied. "My name is Ali. My parents and I are just moving in." He looked back toward the moving truck and nodded toward his mother, who stood on the walkway up to the home, directing three men who carried a large settee across the threshold.

"Habiba," she said to him when he looked back at her. "My name is Habiba. I live here with my parents as well." She laughed lightly. "And my uncle, and my aunt, and their children." She looked down the street, in the direction Hamid's car had gone. "And that was my brother, heading off to school."

When she looked back at Ali, he was nodding at her and still smiling. She liked the way one corner of his mouth turned up a little more than the other.

"And you? Do you go to school?" he asked her.

Habiba shook her head. "No. I help my mother here at home. And take care of my cousins. What do you do?"

"I am part owner of a hotel," he said, the other side of his mouth turning up as well. "Planning to be full owner one day."

Habiba laughed again. "That sounds like a wonderful job."

Ali shrugged. "It pays the bills."

She liked his humility. And his looks. And the way he spoke. And—

"I have to go," Habiba said suddenly, her cheeks flushing once more. She turned and put her hand on the doorknob, ready to go inside.

"Well, I hope we can speak again," Ali said, raising his voice to catch her attention.

It worked. She turned back and smiled at him. "I'm sure we will," she ventured, then she opened the door and stepped inside.

* * *

"Please, eat, eat!" Habiba's mother urged their guests as they all sat around the table, which was piled high with food. The room was alive with laughter and conversations between aunts and uncles, cousins and friends, and most important, the Saids—the family who had just moved in next door. As soon as Habiba's parents had heard they had new neighbors, they went directly over to introduce themselves and to invite the Saids—mother Hajar, father Ahmed, and of course their son, Ali—over to share a meal. This was their way, always to make friends, not enemies.

Habiba, of course, was on kitchen duty, cooking and serving up the many dishes her mother had helped her prepare throughout the day: beef tagine with a wide selection of fresh vegetables, a roasted chicken, and several whole broiled fish. Habiba served the dishes up one by one, her younger female cousins enlisted to carry them to the table. Each time she sent something out, she paused whatever she was doing and stood still, an ear tilted toward the door, listening for the final verdict—an *ooh* or an *aah* that let her know all her hard work had not been in vain. Invariably she heard what she wanted to hear, and then the guests grew silent as they enjoyed the food.

Habiba returned to the stove with a smile. Cooking for a party of a dozen or more was a lot of work, but she couldn't complain. She knew how fortunate they were to have the opportunity to host such a gathering and to feed everyone in this opulent style. They had more than they needed—she thanked Allah every day for that and never forgot all the hard work her father had put in over the years to keep them in this lifestyle. Standing over a hot burner now, stirring a pot of harira, she bowed her head and said a little prayer of gratitude.

"You haven't fallen asleep, have you?"

Habiba looked up quickly at the sound of the young man's voice.

"Ali," she said, feeling that familiar blush come to her cheeks once more. Three of her younger cousins who stood nearby giggled at her behind their hands, and she shot them a glare. "What are you—" she began to say to Ali, but she stopped herself. The load of dishes in his hands let her know exactly why he had come into the kitchen. "How has the food been?" she asked instead, wiping her hands on her apron and turning to face him.

He set the dishes down on the counter next to the sink. "Very good," he replied, smiling at her. "*Very* good. Did you prepare it all yourself?"

"Oh no, my mother and aunts helped earlier in the day. I've just been doing the finishing touches."

He was moving back toward the door; really it was not appropriate for them to be alone, with only the children present. "Well, thank you for all your work," he said, and bowed his head graciously.

Habiba smiled. "It is my pleasure. Enjoy." She nodded at him as well as he backed his way out of the kitchen.

Turning back to her soup with a sigh, Habiba felt an unfamiliar feeling in her chest. It took her a moment, but she realized that it was her heart fluttering.

What are you doing? she asked herself silently. *You don't even know this man.*

Yet there was something about him that made her want to get to know him.

Chapter 3

1971

Habiba turned around and around in front of the full-length mirror. She could not believe this was her looking so . . . so . . . *beautiful*. All her life she had heard others say how pretty she was, how lovely her long hair was, and how brilliant her smile. But she had never seen it in herself until now. She twirled and twirled, her teal and gold silk caftan blooming out around her like the petals of the sweetest flower. Around her neck she wore a thick, intricately constructed necklace of white beads decorated with gold floral medallions, and around her waist a wide belt to match; her wrists clanged and clacked with the ten gold and teal-colored metal bangles she wore. Watching herself in the mirror, she brought her hands up and waved them languidly before her face, admiring the lines, swirls, and patterns of the deep-brown mehndi that decorated the backs and fronts of her fingers and palms. Atop her head sat a gold and diamond crown, an antique white-lace veil flowing from it down to the backs of her knees.

She looked beautiful. She felt beautiful. *And just in time*, she thought. After all, it was her wedding day. She thought for a moment about her husband-to-be, her sweet Ali, getting ready next door at his parents' house. She and Ali had been waiting for this day for a long, long time, and she knew he was probably as nervous and excited as she was. Their courtship had been long by anyone's standards—three years almost, and in all that time they had never been alone once. Following their religious and cultural traditions, they saw each other only when accompanied by members of their families, in groups and at gatherings where they could speak to one another but never share how they truly felt. Still, Habiba knew. She had known from the moment she had first laid eyes on Ali, out in the driveway of his home as he'd carried in boxes from the moving truck.

That will be the man I marry, she had told herself at the time, a fleeting thought that she had barely even dared to think. But that feeling had never left her; in fact it had only grown stronger each time she was in his presence. When she sat next to him—not touching, of course; they had barely even held hands yet—she felt an electricity pass between them, a shock of attraction and admiration, a certain feeling that let her know he was the one. And from the gleam in his eyes when he looked at her, she had always been absolutely certain that he felt the same.

"Habiba," her mother called as she opened the bedroom door, "stop staring at yourself and come out. The photographer is here to take your picture."

She smiled at her mother, who paused in the doorway to admire her daughter. Though she had always been so proud of both of her children—Habiba, her lifelong helper, and Hamid, now in his last year of secondary school and preparing to go to university—at the moment her heart swelled with pride in the stunning young woman who stood before her, holding her arms out to her sides, showing off her dress.

"You look wonderful," Habiba's mother said as her daughter came over to her. She put her hands on Habiba's arms and held them out to get a good view of her. She shook her head and smiled, feeling tears forming against the backs of her eyes. "A year ago, when we began to prepare for your marriage, I envisioned this day, but never . . . never did I think it would turn out to be so grand."

The future bride and groom had begun the process of getting married a year earlier, when their families had gathered together and they'd signed a formal marriage commitment in their presence. It had been a solemn ceremony, pledging not only two people to each other but bringing two families to become one. Ali had brought her gifts, too—sugar, to represent the sweetness of their future life together; milk, representing the purity of their love; and other traditional items such as water and henna and an enormous bouquet of the most fragrant orange flowers. After that he had bestowed upon her his personal gifts, which he had arranged in a large, silver-colored container, like a big tagine—perfumes and bangles, a silk purse, and a satin caftan.

Last of all, and most important, had been the engagement ring. In their only act of physical contact, he had taken her hand in his and slid the cool, gold band onto her finger, its large diamond catching the light from all angles and reflecting it up onto her gleaming face. Habiba looked at it again now. She never took it off, and it was still as lustrous as the day Ali had placed it on her hand.

"Thank you, Mama," Habiba said, leaning in for an embrace. The two women laughed as her mother accidentally tugged on the lace veil a little bit, and it began to pull the crown from Habiba's head. She stepped back, and her mother reached up to resecure it with the hairpins that held it in place.

In the sitting room, the photographer had set up lights and backdrops for her formal portraits. Habiba posed by herself first, then with her female relatives and friends individually and as a group. The other girls and she laughed recalling their hamam only two days earlier—the traditional sauna for a bride-to-be where they sang her songs and participated in the act of purification with her. Habiba had always felt a closeness to the women and girls in her life, a bond they shared based not only on familial or friendly ties but on shared experiences, on the cultural mores underneath which most of them lived. They, too, were not allowed to be educated; they, too, had stayed home all their lives and taken care of their families.

But this did not mean they were lesser than the men in their lives. They might not have gone to universities and they might not have brought home the money that kept their households afloat, but they contributed some of the most invaluable, intangible aspects of family life: the love, the spirit of togetherness, the tenderness only a woman could show to those about whom she cared. These were strong women, intelligent women, and girls who would grow up in the women's' footsteps to be the same. Sitting with them all now in the front room of her parents' home, posing for the photographs that would mark this occasion, when she was about to go and make a new home of her own, she felt this closeness more than ever. No distance between them, she knew, could ever break apart their bonds.

* * *

Habiba had always dreamed of an outdoor wedding in the afternoon, when the sun was low in the sky and cool breezes blew in from the coast nearby, rustling the leaves of the palms. Maybe the ceremony would take place on the beach; maybe it would be in a meadow somewhere, with lush green grass and patches of wildflowers scattered about. The guests' chairs would be draped in dark-pink satin, and matching banners would hang all around the space, rippling in the wind. At the front would be two enormous sprays of roses in every color. Habiba would stand between them with her love, with her soon-to-be husband; they would take each other's hands, and—

"Open your eyes, Habiba," her father whispered as they stood arm in arm at the entrance of the courtyard behind Ali's hotel, and she obeyed his command. Before her lay the courtyard, with its stark white walls and vaulted arches, its intricately carved moldings and its domed, dark-wood roof meant to look like the top of a temple or pagoda. To the east was a stunning view of the sea in the distance, to the west an expansive lawn that was almost like the meadow she had envisioned. Even the roses at the front were like her fantasy flowers come to life.

It was a much bigger space than she remembered, though she had seen it only once, when he had brought her and her parents there to check out the space, to try to judge if it would suffice for their only daughter's wedding. It wasn't a grand palace, but it was large enough for the hundreds of guests that were likely to attend—not just family members but her father's business associates as well as Ali's, whose business had grown exponentially since he had become full owner of the hotel only six months earlier.

And all of them had turned up. *All* of them. Everywhere Habiba looked there were people—in the pink-covered seats and standing against the cloth banners that blew gently in the calm breeze. Women, men, young and old, strangers and the faces she saw every day, and every one of them looking at her. Smiling, expectant, nodding their heads and raising their hands to give her little waves, eager to acknowledge her glances. Never in her life had she had so much attention on her, and it made her shift from foot to foot, uncomfortable to say the least. For a moment she wished she were back at home, wearing her ratty old caftan in which she did her housecleaning, a bucket and a mop in one hand, a laundry basket in the other.

"Habiba, it is time," her father whispered then, and he gave her arm a little tug. At the front of the audience, the imam had finished his reading from the Koran, and the guests had joined him in singing a song in praise of the prophet. The last notes of their voices drifted off into the sunny afternoon air, signaling that the ceremony could begin. "Are you ready?"

She looked at her father, at his kind eyes and warm smile. People told Habiba that she favored him, that she was like him not only in looks but in sentiment. Perhaps this was true; she had inherited his compassion as well as his pointy nose, his easy, uproarious laugh in addition to the cleft in his chin. Her father was a wealthy man, an important man, but he had worked for all he'd earned and had never let any of it change him.

"Humility," he always told his daughter, "is the most important thing you can ever own. Never let your possessions get in the way of it."

"I am ready," she told him, then she took a deep breath and set her foot onto the long, white runner that would bring her to the front of the courtyard, where Ali waited for her, sitting on the Amariya. He smiled as she walked down the aisle toward him, and she focused on nothing else—not the sea of faces around her, not the sound of the band that had begun to play, nothing but the face of the man she loved, the man she would get to spend the rest of her life with, Allah willing. Simply the thought of it sent a flurry of butterflies all through her stomach. When she reached the Amariya, she stepped in and sat down beside Ali, and they looked at one another for a moment, a secret twinkle in their eyes.

"This is it," Ali said, and Habiba could hear the nervousness in his tone. She wanted to reach out and touch his face, to comfort him, to tell him it would be all right. But she hesitated, and then the moment was gone. Four strong men had hoisted the Amariya onto their shoulders, jostling Habiba and Ali as they got their grips right and then began to walk. They did a tour of the room and then another one, making sure everyone had a chance to see the couple, to wish them the utmost of happiness and luck.

When the tour was through, the four men lowered the Amariya to the floor right where they had picked it up originally, leaving Habiba and Ali before the imam again. Now the ceremony could start in earnest. There were more prayers read, more songs sung; Habiba changed her dress a number of times until finally she wore a magnificent white wedding dress, made for her especially by one of Morocco's top designers. As she entered the courtyard for the final time as a single woman, the crowd all ooh'ed and aah'ed, and she blushed as she walked down the aisle to marry the man of her dreams.

Chapter 4

1972

"Oh!"

Habiba sat up in bed, leaning back on her elbow, one hand rubbing the rounded bump of her lower belly.

"What is it?" Ali asked, sitting up as well, his voice and his eyes groggy from sleep.

Habiba laughed and looked at him. "I felt a kick."

"A kick?" Ali asked, sitting up in an instant, his eyes immediately wide open. "Really?"

Habiba laughed again, this time at her husband's innocent sense of wonder. "Yes, really. Here." She took his hand and put it next to hers, on top of the smooth, white satin of her caftan. "Now just wait a moment. We'll see if he does it again."

"He," Ali said, giving her a teasing look. "You always seem so sure of that."

Habiba shrugged and smiled shyly, looking down at her ever-growing midsection. "I don't know why," she replied, "but I feel very strongly that our baby is going to be a boy. Don't you—"

She stopped then, and she and her husband merely looked at one another.

"I felt it," Ali said at last, his voice a whisper, as if speaking any louder might wake the baby. "I felt him kicking!"

Habiba grinned. "*Him*?" she asked, taking on her husband's teasing tone.

Ali lay back down again, the down-filled pillow poufing out as his head hit it rather hard. "Oh, Habiba," he said, sounding exasperated but with a wide smile on his face, "come here."

He held his arms out open to her, and she lay down too, nestling into his embrace, her back against his stomach. She closed her eyes, one hand still holding her belly, as it always seemed to be. No matter what she was doing—shopping at the market, cleaning around the house, visiting with family or friends—her hand was always resting there, as if to soothe her unborn child. In fact, she did it because it calmed her nerves, this reminder of the life growing inside her. It reminded her to slow down, to stop worrying, to take the time to enjoy what she was going through. Soon enough she would be back to hurrying around again—though this time it would be to feed the baby, to change the baby's diaper, to pick the baby up when he or she began to cry.

Now, in bed, her husband's hand joined hers once more, and their fingers entwined over the place where their child rested, waiting to be born. Habiba was only four months pregnant, but it already felt like a lifetime—one she would live over and over if only she could. Pregnancy agreed with her, that was what her mother said. She'd had no morning sickness, no ill side effects at all. She did seem to be hungry all the time, and she needed a nap every afternoon now, but other than that, she felt as right as rain. In fact, she felt happier than she had ever been. She was married to the man of her dreams; they lived in a beautiful home only a few blocks away from their families; and now they were starting a family of their own. Life could not have been much better as far as Habiba was concerned.

This good fortune continued through the coming months. As Habiba's belly swelled, so did her and her husband's joy. To be with child was such a blessing, and so soon after they'd been married. It had taken Habiba only a few months to conceive. She would always remember the day she told Ali that they were expecting their first child. She had just come from her doctor's office, where a blood test had revealed the good news.

"So, I went to my doctor today," she had told Ali as they sat down to dinner that night. "Remember, because I've felt so tired lately?"

He put down the piece of bread he had just broken off from the loaf Habiba had brought home fresh from the bakery. "And what did the doctor say?" His face was a mask of concern. Ever since she had told him she was not feeling well, he had been worried about her.

Habiba had looked down at her folded hands in her lap, smiling shyly. "Well, I am not ill," she began.

Ali had just looked at her. When she did not go on, he made a motion with his hand, urging her to continue.

She had looked up at him, revealing her wide, warm grin. "Ali, I am pregnant," she'd said, then brought her hands up over her mouth, as if she were surprised she had let the secret out.

For a moment her husband had looked at her. "Pregnant?" he asked, as if he had no idea of the word's meaning. "You mean . . . we're . . . going to have a . . . a baby?"

Habiba had laughed and uncovered her mouth, then she reached out and took Ali's hands in hers. "Yes, my dear, yes. We are going to have a baby."

Ali had jumped right up out of his chair. He'd paced the room, one hand on his waist, one on his forehead, a look of grave concern on his face. "There's so much to do," he muttered to himself. "We have to tell our families. And I'll have to arrange to take some time off of work. And the nursery!" He turned to his wife. "Habiba, do you think we should hire a decorator?"

She laughed when she recalled this later, as she stood in the middle of their baby's room, which she had managed to design herself. They could have hired someone if they had wanted to; Ali's hotel was doing enormous business with the growing influx of tourists to the city, and they certainly wanted for nothing. He took great care of his wife, and she had no doubt he would provide very well for their child, too. Still, decorating the nursery felt like something she should do herself—not something she should hand over to a stranger. Habiba and Ali both would be spending a lot of time there once the baby came; might as well, she figured, make it look exactly how they wanted it to look.

By the eighth month, everything seemed to be falling into place. Habiba had been going for her regular doctor visits, and everything was good with both baby and mother. Her own mother, as well as her aunts and female cousins, seemed to be at the house every day, cooking and cleaning for her, making sure she did not overexert herself, and catering to her every whim. Habiba, of course, asked them for nothing, but still they were happy to provide whatever she wished. All she had to do was mention she was thirsty, and a glass of water appeared in her hand as if by magic.

As far as the nursery, she and Ali had decided on lemon-yellow walls and a green carpet, a dark-wood crib and a changing table to match. There were pictures of animals on the walls—childlike cartoons of elephants and lions and giraffes—and a brown-upholstered rocking chair for Habiba. She often stood inside the quiet room, picturing herself sitting in it with her infant, gently rocking the child to sleep, everything around them silent and at peace. Everything perfect. Everything as it should be.

* * *

When the day finally came, Habiba was at home by herself. It was early in the morning; Ali was already at work, and her mother and aunt had not made it over yet, most likely still getting the younger children up and about, sending the boys off to school. Habiba stood in the kitchen, waiting for the tea kettle to whistle, an empty porcelain cup with a tea bag sitting on the counter in front of her. She gazed out the window at the backyard, at the way the trees' leaves swayed in the morning wind.

Finally the kettle sounded, and she reached to turn it off. As she did, though, she felt something shift inside her belly, and a trickle of water started to run down her thigh. She lifted the edge of her caftan and looked at it curiously, for the moment not registering what was about to happen. Then, before her eyes, the trickle turned into a flood, and before she knew what was happening, she was standing in a puddle in the middle of the kitchen floor.

"Ali!" she cried into the phone a moment later, when she had finally reached him at the hotel. "You must come home. My water broke! The baby is on its way!"

The next call was to her mother, who arrived moments before Ali got there. Habiba already had a bag all packed—she'd taken care of that months ago and kept it in the hall closet by the front door, ready in case of emergency. Finally that time had come! As soon as Ali arrived, he picked her up and carried her to the car, gently placed her in the passenger seat, and then went back for her bag. Within twenty minutes, she was checking into the maternity ward at the hospital.

Three hours later, she was holding her baby in her arms.

"Oh, Ali," she whispered, careful not to wake the sleeping

baby, "isn't he the most beautiful thing you've ever seen?"

Her husband gave her a look out the sides of his eyes, picking up on her subtle emphasis on the word *he*.

"Yes," he replied. "And you were right. Our baby is a boy. How did you know all along?"

Habiba shrugged, unable to take her eyes from her child. She ran her fingertip along his perfect little nose, across his tiny, feathery eyelashes. "I have no idea," she said, her voice cracking, tears of love threatening to spill from her eyes. "I just knew."

In keeping with tradition, Habiba let Ali name their firstborn son, and he chose to call the child Mohammed. A regal name, Habiba thought, for a true prince. They would treat him like royalty, like he was the most important child ever born—because to them he was. Mohammed was the sun as it rose in the morning and as it set at night; he was the moon and the stars and all of the galaxies in between. Habiba and Ali hung on his every gurgle and coo, laughing along with him when he smiled, bouncing him in their arms and kissing his warm, fuzzy head whenever he cried.

And as she had imagined she would, Habiba spent hours in that comfortable rocking chair of hers, swaying until her baby fell asleep in her arms, till she was lulled herself into a half-waking state. In those foggy moments, she felt weightless, as if the two of them had somehow drifted right off into the air, tethered to the nursery only by the threads of her dreams, which were always about Mohammed. She was a mother now. And nothing else would fill her thoughts.

Chapter 5

1974

Being a mother changes a woman. Habiba's own mother had always told her as much, but she had never known the truth of it until she had a child herself. Though Habiba had never been self-centered, having Mohammed to care for made her even less so, to the point where she felt as if she lived and breathed only for him, as if she existed for his happiness. Though others might have found this sort of arrangement smothering, Habiba relished it. From the day he had been born, Mohammed had become the most important person in the world to her, and she took his joy seriously. If her son was not happy, neither was she.

Ali, unfortunately, did not seem quite as pleased with the situation.

"It's always Mohammed, Mohammed, Mohammed," he said to her once in a fit of pique. He had come home from work and found her bathing their son, the boy buried in a mound of soap bubbles in the bathtub. Both mother and child were giggling and swatting at the suds to try to uncover him, appearing as if they were having so much fun. Ali had gone through a rather difficult day, and for some reason their gaiety instantly irritated him.

"You never even ask how I am anymore," he told her later, when he had calmed down a bit. "You don't seem to think of me anymore, and it hurts."

Habiba had leaned in and kissed him then, and she could see the concern on his face. She was a good wife—the best, really, always putting his needs and wants ahead of hers. She did not like to see him upset.

"I'm so sorry," she said to him quietly, gazing into his eyes, her brow lowered. "Ali, I will make it up to you."

And she did. For a time, she became more attentive to her husband. She still spoke about their son, of course; this is what parents do: They discuss the well-being of their child. But on top of that she made sure that every day when he came home, she was there to take his coat from him, to hand him a cup of hot tea, to listen to him talk about how his business was doing, about some odd guest they'd had at the hotel, anything that was on his mind. While Mohammed slept or sat in his high chair, splattering pureed vegetables all over himself and the kitchen, Habiba sat at the table with her husband, hanging on his every word and giving him the attention he so sorely needed.

Occasionally, she had to admit, this did annoy her a bit. Ali was a grown man; why was he acting like a petulant child? Mohammed was the baby in the house—he was the one who needed the attention. And it killed Habiba inside a little bit when she had to ignore her son to listen to her husband talk about things he had talked about a thousand times before. Business was doing well or it wasn't; the tourists were a never-ending parade of characters that either delighted or amazed the hotel staff. If he wanted to tell her about these things, why didn't he say so? Why did she have to sit at his feet, begging for him to speak?

She thought about this often, and it was on her mind one morning when the phone rang, around ten o'clock. Ali had long since headed off to work, and Habiba had just put Mohammed down for his first daily nap of the day.

"Hello?" she said when she answered the phone, trying to sound as bright and cheery as possible, in case it was Ali. He disliked when she answered the phone sounding tense or dour.

"Habiba," said the voice on the other end of the line, but it was not her husband. It was her aunt.

"Auntie?" Habiba asked, lowering her brow at the unusual call and the distraught sound of the older woman's voice. "What is it?"

Her aunt sniffled and did not speak for a moment. "Habiba, it's your mother," she finally said, but that was all she managed to get out.

"I'll be right over," Habiba replied and then hung up the phone before her aunt could protest.

Within half an hour, Habiba was at her mother's house. "What is going on?" Habiba asked as her aunt ushered her inside and took the still-sleeping baby from her arms.

Her aunt shook her head, still obviously upset and almost unable to speak. "The doctor said it might have been a stroke, Habiba," she finally whispered quickly, then she shook her head again. "Just go. Go to her."

Habiba did not hesitate. She ran to her mother's room to find her lying in bed, surrounded by Habiba's father, their doctor, and various family members. Habiba went over to her father, who greeted her with open arms.

"How is she doing?" Habiba asked while in her father's embrace.

He pulled away a little and glanced over at his wife, who looked to be asleep. He, too, shook his head. "Habiba, it is not good." His voice broke on the last words, and a flood of tears gushed from his eyes.

Habiba took him back into her arms. "OK," she said to him, patting his back. "OK."

Finally, when his sobbing subsided, he moved away. "Talk to her," he said. "Tell her you love her. She needs to hear these things."

Habiba looked at her mother, lying silent on the bed. "Can she ... will she be able to hear me?"

Her father dabbed at his eyes with a handkerchief he had pulled from his pants pocket. "Nobody knows," he said, then he took a deep breath. "But it can't hurt, Habiba."

"No," she replied, "of course not." And then she automatically moved to her mother's side. Kneeling down on the floor beside the bed, she took her mother's hand in her own. It was cold and limp, as if the life had already gone out of it. Still, her mother's chest continued to rise and fall—the only sign that she was still with them in body, if not in spirit.

"Mama," Habiba whispered, moving her lips close to her mother's ear. Immediately tears sprang to her eyes, and she did not know what to say. That she loved her mother, of course, that always went without saying. That was always obvious in the thousands of little ways they cared for one another on a day-to-day basis, in their quick conversations and their serious talks about what it meant to be a wife, a mother, a woman in this culture in which they lived. Habiba's mother had taught her so much, from the time she was a small girl, so many things she could not have learned at any school. She might not have been formally educated, but her mother's teachings had brought to her a wisdom that could not be bought or sold, that could exist nowhere other than in the realm of women.

"Mama," she said again, moving in even closer until she could feel her mother's hair brushing against her face. "Mama, I love you."

And that was all she managed to get out. Because as soon as she said it, her mother's body racked with a great gasp, and everyone in the room stopped what they were doing. All eyes moved to the bed, where her mother's body lay still again, this time no breath going in or out. An eternity seemed to pass, and then slowly the air hissed back out of her throat, a long, slow exhale that ended in a gurgling cough.

And just like that, Habiba's mother was gone.

* * *

They say that when a wife dies, it's sometimes nearly impossible for the husband to remain tethered to this earth, and that was certainly the case for Habiba's father. After her mother passed, her father roamed around their house as if it were an empty shell; he did not go to work, he did not eat, and she could tell from the look in his eyes that he barely slept as well. He was a zombie, a living dead person himself, walking as if in two worlds: the one that was real and the one where he imagined himself still living with his wife, his beloved who had gone and left him all alone. He could not take the grief of it, and, some said later, that was finally what did him in. Habiba's father passed in his sleep some three months after her mother died. There was no known cause of death other than a broken heart.

Chapter 6

1976

"What is this?"

Habiba looked at Ali, unsure exactly what his question meant. In his hand he held a long, white paper—the receipt from her shopping trip at the local supermarket earlier in the day. She'd spent a couple of hours there with Mohammed, choosing foods for a special meal she had planned to prepare for Ali that evening—something to cheer him up, since he'd seemed to be in such a foul mood lately. Problems at work again, she figured, though every time she asked him about it, he said he didn't want to talk. In truth he seemed more annoyed by her attempts at kindness than anything else.

"Looks like the receipt from the market," she said as she put Mohammed into his high chair. "Why do you ask?"

When Ali did not answer her, she turned around to look at him and was alarmed by what she saw. His eyes were blazing, his hair a mess, and he was gripping the receipt so hard, his knuckles had turned all white.

"How much did you spend?" he asked her, his voice low and threatening.

Habiba felt goose bumps work their way up her back. She had seen Ali angry before; he was only human, after all, and sometimes he did lose his temper with her. He would raise his voice; sometimes he would slam a door, and once he put a cup down on the table so forcefully, it broke into several pieces. But none of that had scared her, not like his demeanor right now, that look in his eyes and the tone of his voice.

However, she tried to laugh it off, to defuse the situation before it got any worse—like she always did. "Well, it says right there on the receipt, dear," she told him. "Here, right at the bottom—"

She reached for the slip of paper, but he pulled it back quickly so she couldn't reach it. He continued to glare at her so hard she had to look away. She focused her eyes down to the floor.

"I forget exactly how much I spent," she said at last, keeping her voice meek and mild. "But it does say right there, if I could just look at it—"

"You don't need to look at anything!" Ali roared at her, taking the receipt in both of his hands and ripping it to shreds as he continued. "You know very well how much of my hard-earned money you're throwing away on things that we don't need."

"Things we don't need?" she asked, unable to hold her tongue. "Ali, I was buying food for—"

Once again he would not allow her to finish. "And how long were you out today, hmm?" he asked, taking a step closer toward her.

"I . . . I . . . ," Habiba stuttered, surprised by the question. The supermarket was one of the few places she went anymore, aside from her family's house. Ali had forbade her from most other places—even the park, where she used to take Mohammed for walks. "I wasn't that long," she replied, still unsure what the question meant.

"I tried calling you for two hours!" Ali shouted at her, so vehemently that drops of spit flew off his lips at her. "Two hours, Habiba! What were you doing out for that long? Where were you? Who were you with?"

Again she laughed a little, but only from nerves; she couldn't help it. "I was with the baby," she said, looking back at Mohammed, who was looking between his parents, obviously wondering which one of them was going to feed him. Remembering that was what she had come into the kitchen to do, she moved to the refrigerator, where she found a container of strained carrots. She set it in a pot to warm it up, feeling Ali's eyes on her back with every move she made.

"I asked you where you were," he said at last, when she turned away from the stove. "And I asked who you were with."

His tone of voice had gone calm but too much, Habiba thought. He sounded like he was controlling himself from spiraling off into a fearsome rage.

"I was at the supermarket," she said just as calmly, trying to keep the tremor of the fear she felt out of her voice. "And the only person I was with was Mohammed. We did the shopping, and we came right home."

"That is a lie!" Ali yelled, and before Habiba knew what he was doing, he was in front of her, his strong hand gripping her thin wrist.

"Ali, please stop," she said, trying to wriggle herself free. "You're hurting me."

"Oh, I'm hurting you, am I?" he asked, then he tightened his grip on her wrist so hard she was sure it was going to leave a mark.

She looked him in the eyes then, and for a moment she saw a flash of their wedding day, standing in front of those hundreds of people, looking into Ali's eyes, so excited about their future together. She had been so sure he was the one, so positive that their life would be one of unadulterated bliss.

And it had been, up to a point. She could never quite put her finger on exactly when these bad moods of his had started, or exactly why. All she knew was that more and more, when he came home from work, he seemed angry at her, and she could never figure out why. His business was great; in fact he had just started construction on another hotel and resort, since his first one was doing so well. They had their baby, their home, and by all accounts their life should have been one of easy pleasure.

Instead it had turned into this difficult thing. Habiba had been able to manage his moods for a while, appeasing him with food and drink, by rubbing his feet after a particularly long day, by serving him in any way he wanted and any way she could dream. This seemed to keep him happy enough. But after awhile, even a doting wife was not enough for him. Her attention seemed to annoy him. If she brought him his slippers, he batted them away. Her food tasted like dirt, and her attempts at light conversation sounded idle and inane. Worst of all he was never hesitant to tell her any of this.

"Yes, Ali, you're hurting me," she said now, hearing the whimpering sound in her own words. "Please stop." All she wanted was to be let free, and if it took a little begging, so be it.

But her tactic did not work. Instead he tightened his grip again.

"Shut up!" he screamed at her, his open mouth directly in front of her face. "Just stop talking, Habiba! When will you ever learn just to keep your mouth shut?"

And with that, he pulled his arm back and let it go, delivering a slap across her face that left a terrible sting. Without thinking she brought her own hand up to where he had hit her. The skin was warm and tender and, likely, growing red.

His rage spent, Ali backed away from her, wiping his mouth on the back of his shirt sleeve. He did not take his eyes from her. He was not ashamed of what he had done.

Across the room, in his high chair, Mohammed started at once to bawl, and Habiba automatically went right over to him. She picked him up and set him on her hip, holding on to him with both arms and bouncing him up and down. On the stove the pot with the strained carrots was beginning to boil. She went over and turned it off then turned to look at her husband. He was standing before the open refrigerator, bending over as if to see what they had to eat, as if nothing out of the ordinary had happened in the least.

Habiba stared at him for a moment, a thought forming in her mind. As soon as her thought became clear, she took her baby and marched across the kitchen, toward the door.

Ali stood up straight and closed the refrigerator door. "Where do you think you're going?" he asked her.

She stopped in the doorway and turned around, holding tightly to Mohammed. "I'm going to my aunt's house," she told her husband calmly, her chin held high. "And you'd better not expect me ever to come back."

Chapter 7

1977

Habiba went to the only place she knew would welcome her, where no one would question a young woman leaving a rich, successful husband like Ali. Her brother Hamid had moved into their childhood home after their father had passed away. His studies at university had paid off and he, too, was young and successful. He had also mellowed with age; gone was the moody child Habiba had doted on, replaced by a wise young man with their mother's features.

She could not hide her distress when she walked through the door, and Hamid was instantly at her side to comfort her. "What's wrong?" he asked. "What's happened?"

Habiba told him everything. Her brother was surprised that Ali had become such a distrustful tyrant. He wanted to do something but knew his sister had few rights. He did the only thing he knew he could do. "Welcome home!" he said, opening his arms wide.

Habiba was flooded with relief and could not stop herself from crying tears of joy. She fell into her brother's arms and held Mohammed close to her. Hamid kissed the tops of both of their heads and patted his sister's shoulder. "It's okay," he whispered into her ear. "It's going to be all right." She believed him and knew she would be forever grateful for her brother's love, courage, and acceptance.

He lived by himself in their old house. All of the younger cousins had gotten married and were living with families of their own or had moved away to school or work. Their aunt and uncle now lived with the oldest cousin, his wife, and their two children. Habiba would live on the second floor, and the third floor would be Mohammed's new nursery. She knew she would never be able to repay him, but Hamid would not hear such talk. "You are my sister and I love you," he would tell her again and again. "Whatever you need, I will provide."

The joy of returning home, of being back with her beloved brother flooded her soul! Habiba could hardly believe it. Her life now was like her childhood all over again. Hamid would spend his days at work, but the rest of the day they were together. When they weren't doting on each other, they would both spend all their efforts on baby Mohammed. Habiba did not have to live in fear of anyone's jealousy; they both loved her son equally and more than anyone.

Hamid loved playing with Mohammed and making his nephew laugh. Hamid would cover his face and make funny faces for Mohammed. He would bounce the boy on his knees or throw him into the air to catch him. Habiba would playfully scold her brother when it was time to feed her son or put him to bed. "You can't have him all the time," she said, and they would laugh.

There was no word from Ali to bring her back, no attempt to heal their family. They briefly worried that he might try to harm her reputation, but nothing was done. No one heard from him, and Habiba was glad to be under his thumb no longer. "It's too bad how it ended, after it began so well," she lamented to Hamid one day.

"I suppose marriage changes people," he said simply.

When Mohammed turned three, he became much more

of a handful. He no longer took the unsteady steps of a toddler and instead raced about the house. Habiba and Hamid had their hands full keeping after him, trying to keep him out of trouble or from injuring himself by running into something or falling. When he did bump his head on the wall or a piece of furniture, Habiba was there to kiss away his tears and hold him tight. His uncle would make another silly face or a funny sound, and soon Mohammed had forgotten what troubled him in the first place.

Eventually, Hamid had big news to share of his own. "I have met someone. Her name is Faiza and she is the most beautiful woman I have ever seen." He could hardly contain his happiness. "I visited with her parents yesterday evening and asked if I could have her hand in marriage. They said yes!"

He was smiling so brightly that Habiba tried hard to hide her initial feelings of misgiving. "I'm so happy for you! That's wonderful news! You must love her very much."

"I do, Habiba," he said, nodding his head vigorously. "I have admired her from afar for a very long time. I didn't dare tell anyone about my feelings, not even you, because I worried nothing would come of them." He laughed. "I suppose that seems silly now."

"It does. Who would not love you, my brother?" Habiba smiled brightly and gave his shoulder a squeeze. "When will the wedding take place?"

"Right away! Her parents seemed anxious to cement our union as soon as possible."

At this, Habiba could no longer contain what was troubling her. "What about us?" she asked. "What about Mohammed and me? Are we still welcome here? Does she know that we are living with you?"

"She does, and it doesn't matter. There's plenty of room in

this house for all of us." He wanted to do his best to reassure her. "I told you that you are welcome here, and that will never change."

* * *

Faiza was as beautiful as Hamid had said she was. Her skin was burnished, and her hair was long and flowed like water down her back. Her eyes were deep and had a piercing quality to them that Habiba found almost unsettling. Unfortunately, they were often used to criticize her.

"Why can't you help out more around the house? Am I to do all the cleaning like a servant in my own home?" Faiza would ask such questions of Habiba nearly every day, no matter how often she washed dishes or did laundry or cleaned. Her sister-in-law also refused to help with Mohammed. "He is not my child, so he is not my responsibility," she often said with a haughty turn of her head.

Hamid's wedding felt like a blur, like a period of weeks that had passed so long ago because everything had happened so fast. Her brother's in-laws hadn't been kidding about the marriage happening as quickly as possible. Their courtship was barely a few months before the wedding took place with great festivities.

Habiba felt sick for days leading up to the wedding and wasn't able to attend. She also didn't want Mohammed running around and potentially causing chaos, so she mostly stayed away from any planning. The first time she met Faiza was when she moved in.

They had clashed almost immediately. When Habiba greeted Faiza, her sister-in-law lifted her chin and looked down her nose in a gesture that quickly became far too familiar. "It is nice to meet you, sister," she said coldly. Habiba could not help but doubt her sincerity.

Hamid could see that there was discord in his home but was unsure how to fix it. When Faiza complained about how Habiba would not help around the house, he would explain that she had a child to raise. "Why are you always taking her side?" his wife would shout back at him. She would pout and become withholding.

Habiba did not understand why they could not be a happy family. One day, after she put Mohammed down for a nap, she approached Faiza to try to understand what was going on and to try and work through their differences. "I think there has been a misunderstanding between us somehow. I know my brother loves you very much, but I feel you dislike me. Can we not be friends?"

"Why should we be friends?" Faiza asked. "Hamid told me of your presence here before we married. How you left a rich and powerful husband because he was a little jealous and hit you once. I said it was fine because I wanted to marry Hamid. I wanted a rich and powerful husband of my own."

"Is that why you married my brother? He is not that rich, nor is he that powerful."

"Does he not own this house? Did he not inherit your father's sawmill?" These things were true, but Habiba did not understand. "Do you think I am the only woman who noticed these things? He is a fat, temperamental man. We all remember what he was like as a boy. But when I noticed him looking at me, I took advantage of it. Better to marry a stupid man than remain poor and desperate for the rest of my life."

Habiba was confused by all that Faiza said. It sounded like she was rambling and wasn't making any sense. "What are you saying? Do you not love my brother?"

Faiza did not answer the question but said simply, "I will not let you undermine me in my own home. This house will be mine."

The next day, Hamid approached Habiba. He seemed nervous but also like he needed to speak with her. "Is everything okay?" she asked.

"No," he said with great anguish. "I have just heard the most terrible things. Faiza told me that you have been saying the most awful things about me. She says you call me fat and stupid. She says you accuse her of marrying me for money and that she does not really love me! Please, Habiba, why would you say such things?"

Habiba was shocked. "I did not say such things! I would never say such things. You are my brother and I love you. Do you think I am not grateful for all the things you've done for me?" She hesitated. She did not want to tell Hamid that Faiza had been the one to say such things. She did not want to say anything bad about the woman that her brother clearly adored. In the end, all she could say was, "Please believe me." Hamid left her without another word.

The tension in the house was not addressed again for several months and in that time only got worse. Faiza eventually stopped helping around the house at all but would complain to Hamid that Habiba was sabotaging her efforts to help. Mohammed became anxious and cried at the slightest provocation, worried that a fight would result between his mother and his uncle or aunt.

After several months of this, Habiba awoke to find Hamid in her room. He was standing at the foot of her bed and Faiza was in the corner. "What's going on?" she asked.

"As if you didn't know, you thief!" Faiza shouted. This woke Mohammed, who started to cry and call for his mother.

"Please, Faiza," Hamid begged. "You said you wouldn't say anything."

"I'm sorry, husband. I'm just so angry that she would take advantage of you like this." She struck a defiant pose.

"What's going on?" Habiba asked again. She wanted to go to her son but couldn't move. She did not like what was happening here.

"If you needed money, all you had to do was ask. I would give you anything!" Hamid's voice caught in his throat. He didn't seem capable of continuing for a moment but found his voice. "I noticed money was missing from my wallet earlier. Did you take it, Habiba?"

"Don't you dare lie!" Faiza said.

"Faiza," Hamid said desperately, "can you leave us alone? I will do as I have said I would, I promise." She turned up her nose but after a few moments walked out of the room.

Habiba realized what was happening and couldn't believe it. "You don't think I took your money, do you? Why would I do such a thing?"

Tears streamed from Hamid's face. "I don't know, sister. But Faiza said she saw you take it. And I just found the money here in your dresser!"

"Faiza must have taken it!" Habiba cried out desperately. "You must believe me!" She started to cry herself and fell on her face before her brother. She wanted to keep telling him to believe her but could say nothing over the sobs racking her body.

"I cannot believe that my sister is a thief," Hamid said. "But I cannot believe that my wife is a liar. What am I to do? I cannot continue living this way!" He balled his hands into fists and put them to his temples. "I have no choice, Habiba! There is nothing else I can do."

Habiba looked up and tried crawling to the edge of the bed. She shook her head furiously, refusing to accept what her brother was about to say. After things had been so wonderful, how could they have become so horrible? Mohammed continued to cry and shriek but received no comfort.

"I'm sorry," Hamid said and turned away. "I need to ask you to leave."

Chapter 8

1977

Habiba went to live with her cousin Issam. It took some adjusting, but they were all happy living together. Issam and his wife already had three children, so Mohammed finally had playmates his own age. They would play and laugh together. Habiba was happy that things had settled down in such a way after the turmoil of the last few years. She was ready to go to work and put Mohammed in school.

It was not accepted that a woman should work, of course. Habiba should have stayed with her husband, no matter how much he beat her. She should have let him do all the work and take care of her, no matter how awful her life would have been or how much danger her son would have been in. This is what society deemed as correct. She felt blessed by God that her family would take her in, but she did not want to stay with them without contributing. As much as Habiba would help Issam's wife take care of their children, she wanted to get a job.

She thought she could work at a local store, helping out somehow with sales or greeting customers. She knew it would be difficult. In fact, the first few places she went did not even acknowledge that she was looking for work. They insisted she must be a customer because she was a woman. Habiba did not let this frustrate her. Her life was going to become stable, her son would grow up happy, and she would not let anyone discourage her. It was the most fulfilled she had felt since being reunited with her brother.

She asked Issam's wife about schools, since their oldest child had started attending last year. Her cousin-in-law was not helpful, which was strange. She only provided vague answers and would not look Habiba in the eye. When Habiba became insistent, the only answer she got was, "Talk to Issam!"

Habiba realized talking with her cousin was unavoidable. If nothing else, she wanted to know why his wife was acting so strangely. Issam sighed deeply and looked dismayed. "I did not want you to find out this way," he said.

"Find out what?" she asked.

"My wife is pregnant. We are having another baby." Issam's forehead remained creased as he said this and there was no joy in his voice.

"But that is terrific news!" She laughed lightly and clapped her hands. A wave of relief washed over her. No wonder Issam's wife had acted the way she had! Being pregnant for the fourth time could cause all sorts of strange behavior, Habiba imagined.

"You do not understand," Issam continued. "With this new child, there will be no more room for you and Mohammed. You will no longer be able to stay here once it arrives."

All the color drained from her face and she felt weak in the knees. To go from such happiness to such degradation was too much to bear! The wave of relief had become an undertow of despair. Habiba realized there was nothing for her to stand for and she sank to her knees on the floor. "Please," was all she could say.

He grew sterner and harder upon seeing his cousin on the floor. "Do not make this harder than it has to be. You have nine months." He added under his breath, "If the baby is not premature." He held out his hand. "Get up. Do not let your son see you this way."

The thought of Mohammed made her gather her strength and stand. She did not take her cousin's outstretched help. "You have already made up your mind, haven't you?" she asked in amazement. "There is nothing I can say, no offer I can make to try and change your mind. I cannot convince you based on what I can contribute to this house, or invoke compassion on my son who will start school."

"We have a large family," he said. "I'm sure you'll find someone." He stormed off. Once more, Habiba was left in the retreating shadow of a family member casting her off.

Mohammed took the news surprisingly well. She worried that he was becoming used to a life where they moved frequently, but she didn't let that show. Instead, she made a game of packing up their belongings and trying to find a place to go. Her closest cousins in Casablanca all had families larger than Issam's and could not help her. Eventually, Habiba found a childless aunt and uncle who would let them stay for a few months. It was better than nothing, and she secretly hoped to convince them to let her and Mohammed stay longer. When Issam and his family returned from the hospital with their newest member, she and Mohammed were already gone.

The aunt and uncle's home was the smallest one they had stayed in so far. Even with no other children, the four of them always felt in each other's way. Habiba and Mohammed shared a room, one of only five in the whole house. There were no other floors and only one bathroom for all of them.

Habiba was still optimistic that she would be able to stay longer. She thought she might try to get a job and contribute to the household while enrolling Mohammed in school. Surely, she thought, her aunt and uncle would not throw them out onto the street if it meant taking a young boy out of school.

As she began her job search once more, she felt lightheaded and hurried home. She did not know what was wrong but felt the need to lie down. She ended up staying in bed for three days, unable to move. She did not know what was wrong and tried to put on a brave face. Her aunt recommended home remedies and soups, but these did nothing for her. Finally, they called a doctor who said that he could find nothing wrong with her. She was simply under a strain or exhausted, he said, and should be back to normal within the week. Her aunt and uncle did not change their minds about when she and Mohammed had to leave.

As soon as Habiba was strong enough, she packed up what little was left of her and Mohammed's belongings and moved on. They went from relative to relative, sometimes literally begging for just a few days' rest. Mohammed missed the deadline to start school and ended up taking care of his mother most of the time. She tried to put on a brave face, but he could tell she was in great pain.

The anxiety of having to move and find shelter did not help Habiba, and her condition continued to deteriorate. She grew old before her time and her once great beauty faded under all of her hardship. Her hair turned gray prematurely, and the ache in her bones caused her to move slowly, like someone twice or three times her age. Mohammed would do his best to help her, carrying things for her when they went shopping, cooking meals when she could not, and making tea and helping her to bed when she needed rest.

When he was only six years old, he did what his mother had so often tried to do but could not. He would have to go to work. They needed money and there was no way for him to go to school. They had no permanent address, no way to account for themselves, and no school would accept Mohammed as a student. He could not prove that he knew what he was supposed to have learned, even though he had worked so hard for so long. He went out looking for a job.

He ended up in a factory working to make clothes. He was smaller than other boys his age and could fit inside machinery to fix things, working where no one else could or dared to because of possible unsafe conditions. When he grew to be too big to do this, he tried to stay in the factory as a machinist or handyman. But it was easier for the owner to pay several smaller children a fraction of the cost of promoting Mohammed. He decided to find work elsewhere.

This was their life for the next several years. Every so often, Mohammed would see other children happily playing or going to school. He wished, sometimes desperately so, that he could have been like them. He wanted to live a normal, happy life. Part of him wanted to resent his mother for the life he was living instead, to blame her for the difficulties they were both struggling to endure. He would not listen to the tiny voice inside his head. He loved his mother and was absolutely devoted to her. He was dedicated to helping her as best he could, no matter what the personal toll it took on him. He could see that the toll it took on her was worse.

One day, Mohammed came home after a long day at work. He was working as a tour guide at this time. Tall for his age, many tourists assumed he would know enough to help them around. He did the best he could and worked mainly for tips. He and his mother were living with a distant relative—a great aunt or a second cousin, Mohammed wasn't sure. He ran to his mother's bedside to make sure she was comfortable; she was increasingly frail. He was going to spend his night working for a salvage yard. Before he left, he made sure she was okay. On the table next to her was a small box with a bow on it. Before Habiba fell asleep, she pushed the box toward her son. It was a present for his twelfth birthday.

Chapter 9

1992

Mohammed's twentieth birthday was a much happier time. They had been living with the family of one of his friends for years by then. Mohammed had continued to be a friendly boy, and all of the children he worked with enjoyed his company. One of the children from the factory had five brothers and sisters. When the oldest one had gotten married, they had room to invite Mohammed and Habiba to stay. Habiba had been speechless with gratitude. She tried her best to repay this kindness but was told to rest and recover.

As the years passed, Habiba's health improved, though she was still sometimes wracked with pain from all her years of hardship. Her hair did not regain its luster, nor did her skin become smooth again, but there was a light in her eyes that had threatened to go out many times, and Mohammed was happy to see it again.

They had never been able to send Mohammed to school, unfortunately. He had been too far behind by the time they moved in with his friend's family and could not afford to get him caught up. Mohammed was at peace with this decision. He had plenty of friends and a good job by now. Why did he need to go to school to learn things that did not matter? He already had all the practical skills he needed. He had gone back to the clothing factory and was a supervisor in charge of two floors of workers. He helped improve the efficiency and the profitability so they no longer had to depend on children to work in dangerous situations.

Everyone admired and respected Mohammed, which is part of why his friend was thankful to have him stay with his family. He had one older sister, an older brother, and two younger brothers still living with them. The youngest would be able to go to school instead of work!

The oldest sister had not gone to school, of course, but was able to read. Her brothers would share with her what they learned. Habiba reflected on how much times had changed in Morocco from when she was a girl. This girl's name was Latifa, and she turned eighteen shortly after Mohammed turned twenty. Her hair was a light shade of brown, and her eyes were dark and brooding. They lit up whenever Mohammed was around, though.

It soon became clear to Habiba that the feelings Latifa had for Mohammed were mutual. She would make his lunch for him when he left for work, telling Habiba to rest. When Mohammed came home at the end of the day, he went out of his way to thank her; he somehow knew she had started making his meals instead of his mother. Whenever the family gathered, they sat together. This was accepted, though technically not allowed. Mohammed was seen as a member of the family and allowed to be near Latifa. Besides, they were not alone.

Habiba wanted her son to be happy more than anything else in the world. Now that he was old enough, he deserved a good wife to provide for him the things that she had tried so hard to give him while he was growing up. "Why don't you and Latifa take a walk together tomorrow night? One of her brothers can accompany you," she suggested to him.

He tried to hide his eagerness at accepting the idea but

clearly enjoyed it. Habiba went to Latifa's parents to offer the idea so it would not appear to break any of the rules of their society that were still very much in place so many years after her own courtship of Ali.

She did not ask her son about his time with Latifa but could tell he was happy. This continued for several months. She was not surprised when he said he intended to ask Latifa's parents if they could be married. Habiba could hardly contain her happiness. Of course, Latifa's parents said yes. They had all been living as one family for so long, it only seemed natural to bring their families together. And Latifa and Mohammed were clearly very much in love.

The wedding was to take place in three months at a nearby courtyard. They could not afford much, but it would be beautiful. The only thing that cast a shadow on this incredibly happy time was a conversation Habiba overheard Latifa have with one of her brothers. Habiba was resting because she was tired but had not yet fallen asleep. She heard the younger brother ask, "So will Habiba live with you and Mohammed when you marry and move into your own house?"

All Latifa said in response was, "She will not live with us."

Habiba did not understand. Had she been seen as a burden all this time? Even after all that had happened? They had all been so welcoming and kind. Had they been lying to her face? Would she not live with her own son and his new wife? This was expected. It was tradition! She wanted to find out what was going on but was still so tired. She fell into an uneasy and fitful sleep.

When she awoke, it was later than she expected. She decided not to pursue the thoughts that had so disturbed her. She may have been mistaken in what she heard. Or perhaps Latifa was letting off steam; new brides were often under a great deal of pressure, especially from other members of their own families. Habiba decided not to let her worries interfere with what would be a perfect day and the dawn of the happiest time in her family's life.

The ceremony was beautiful. There were songs, prayers, and much love poured out from the entire community. Everyone brought food, enough for days, and had a wonderful time. Habiba was so full of joy, she could hardly stop herself from crying the whole time. Mohammed looked so happy and proud, wearing the finest garments he'd ever had. They had been given to him by the owner of the factory, along with a silver tea set for their new home.

Their search for a new home had been put on hold for the ceremony but began again shortly thereafter. It was difficult. They could not afford a home, but even a floor or set of rooms in Casablanca was proving to be too expensive. In the end, Mohammed and Latifa had to settle on a single room to rent far away from the rest of the family. There was no room for anyone else. "There is barely room for the two of us," Latifa explained.

Habiba wondered if her daughter-in-law had planned it this way. They could have found something with room for her in addition to the two of them. They could have used some of the influence Mohammed was acquiring, or sold one of their many wedding presents. Latifa was settling for a single room too easily. She would not say anything to Mohammed, of course. She did not want to mar his happiness in any way.

On the day he and his new wife moved out, Mohammed tried to encourage his mother. "You can stay with Latifa's family for as long as you need to. Soon we will have a large house with plenty of room for you and the grandchildren I expect we'll be giving you very soon!"

Habiba smiled and nodded politely. She missed her son terribly after he moved out, but there was not much she could do. They lived far away and she could not make the trip to visit him that often. She did not want to continue living with the family of Mohammed's friends when he was not there. She felt like too much of a burden and began to doubt how welcome she was. After only a few months, she decided to move on.

Chapter 10

1998

Habiba was sick. The exhaustion she felt living with Latifa's family was soon replaced with constant pain, as though someone were stabbing her in the back and sides, when she wasn't doubled over with cramps. She had suffered infections and diseases. She had been to the hospital for kidney problems but did not always know what was wrong with her.

She was living with a distant cousin at this point, an older woman named Najat who had never married. She was older than Habiba by a few years but looked much younger. She had cared for her parents, Habiba's aunt and uncle, for many years before they had died. Najat understood the bond of family and the responsibility of one person to another. When Habiba had come to her, she was grateful for the company more than anything else.

Najat had been the one to suggest going to the doctor. It turned out Habiba had kidney stones and needed surgery. The stones were too large to even consider letting her pass them. "Why wasn't she brought to the hospital months ago?" the doctor had asked. Najat tried to explain that Habiba had not been living with her for long, that she was a relative whose son had abandoned her. He seemed disinterested.

"Do not say Mohammed abandoned me," Habiba had weakly reprimanded. "It was not his fault."

Najat had said nothing. She knew her cousin did not want to make trouble and took too much on herself. Her young loveliness had faded to a meekness that seemed unbecoming. There was still a light of kindness in her eyes, though.

That had been five years ago. In the intervening time, Habiba was sick several more times. The kidney with the stones was eventually removed. "You will eventually get used to life with one kidney," the doctor had reassured her. Mohammed had come to the hospital once to check on her, but she had been asleep. He did not stay and never came back. She'd had no other visitors.

Recovery was long and painful. When Habiba was able to stand and walk on her own, it was with a slow and awkward shuffle. She had found it difficult to speak for a while, but her strength returned after a time. She did not expect to be back to her old self and still felt tired all the time. When she returned to the doctor, he sent her to a specialist who ordered several tests and x-rays. The diagnosis came back: cancer.

Habiba was scared, but Najat helped her through it. She was starting to look older now as well; her hair was beginning to turn gray at the temples, and her face had more lines around her mouth and eyes. She promised to take care of Habiba as best she could.

The treatments were harsh and ravaged Habiba's body. She was nauseous and tired even more now and sometimes needed to be physically carried to perform basic bodily functions. She spent most of her time in a wheelchair. That was the only way she could move, but most of the time she was too sick to push herself.

In spite of how much worse this medicine seemed to make Habiba's condition, the doctors eventually told her that the tumors inside her had become smaller and could be operated on. They wasted little time because of how this was affecting Habiba. There was also the possibility that the cancer would spread even with the operation, but they were willing to take that chance. Her quality of life was slipping rapidly and they wanted to preserve the years she had left.

In the end, she needed two operations—one to remove most of her liver, which had developed cancer that was threatening to spread to her blood. One doctor told her that she could live without most of her liver, using almost the same language as the doctor who had reassured her about the loss of her kidney. The second was to remove a tumor on a bone in her arm. Thankfully, they had caught both in time. Habiba continued to undergo treatments, and the cancer was not spreading.

It was many months before Habiba could walk on her own again. Her hair was thin and her cheeks were sallow. When she was well enough to leave the hospital, the nurses explained that she had to be on a strict diet. She could have no refined sugars, no fat, and no red meat. Her food would have to be prepared a special way to make sure it was not contaminated with anything that might make her sick. Most foods would make her sick now.

Najat brought Habiba home from the hospital but appeared anxious and haggard. Habiba asked her if anything was wrong, but she simply shook her head. There was tension in the air for a few hours. Najat left to go to the store; she needed to buy new groceries to accommodate Habiba's new dietary restrictions. However, on her way to the door, Najat slumped to the floor and sobbed.

Habiba could see her but wasn't sure if her cousin knew she could be seen. She was clearly trying to keep herself composed, but suddenly her cries rang out, "I have spent my life caring for others," she said in a barely audible voice. "Where is my help?

When do I get to live my life? How much must I sacrifice?" She continued to weep and then released a mournful groan. "I cannot do this anymore!"

Habiba knew there would only be confrontation and pain in the future if she continued to live with Najat. With her cousin lying prostrate on the floor, she gathered up what little she owned and snuck out the back of the house. She did not look back.

Chapter 11

1999

The rain was bad that night. Habiba was huddled next to a building. She no longer hoped to become dry or warm. She wasn't even looking to avoid the rain anymore. She just needed an out-of-the-way spot to fall asleep. She thought she might pass out soon from exhaustion or pain. It had been so long since she last slept anyway. Whenever she came close to losing consciousness, the rain lashed at her face and woke her up. She did not know what she would do for the rest of the night.

The last year had been the hardest yet. She had not been back to the hospital because she couldn't afford additional medical care. She knew it would only be bad news anyway and was scared to hear all the things that could be wrong with her. She also had no address to provide, should anyone ask for one, and one was usually required in order to be admitted at the local hospital.

When she left Najat's house, she had walked through the streets of town until, around nightfall, she found another relative who could possibly let her rest. She had found the home of an uncle from her father's side. He was surprised to see her, but her exhaustion was evident. He let her stay for a night but told her she had to leave in the morning. He explained, "I still work and don't want to leave you alone in an empty house. You understand, yes?" Habiba had understood all too well and did not return.

She would walk for days at a time around the city, looking for a friend or relative who might allow her the chance to get a hot meal and a good night's rest. If she was fortunate, she could take a bath and be given some fresh clothes to take with her. Usually, this did not happen. Sometimes they pretended to be happy to see her but would explain that they had no room. Others would be openly hostile or contemptuous. It was the will of Allah that she was destitute and she should know better than to bring her shame and misfortune to their house. Some even saw her as an ill omen, a curse or pestilence that would bring hard times with her.

When Habiba could find no charity among family or friends, she would sleep on the street and beg for food from passersby. It did not occur to her that this act was humiliating or dirty; she was too hungry and desperate. The pain in her insides would force her to her knees, which made it easy for people to ignore her. Sometimes she would sleep where she lay, moving if people kicked her but otherwise too tired to move.

She tried to find charity near the marketplace and business centers of town but was quickly chased off by police, workers, or sometimes total strangers who would not let her try and find sustenance. Now she could not even approach these parts of town without someone telling her she was not welcome there. She walked during the day as long as she would be able to, trying to find a friendly face or a sympathetic ear to at least hear her pleas before politely refusing to help.

Once, delusional with heat and malnutrition, she collapsed in front of a stranger's house. She thought it might have been Mohammed's house even though she hadn't seen her son in years. A young man opened the door and she asked if he were her grandson. The young man, frightened, got his father. She could see he was not her son and realized with terror her mistake. She explained what had happened and implored him not to call the police or to send her away angrily. "If I may take but one moment to gather my strength, I promise I will go away and never return!"

Thankfully, this man took pity on her. He set up a cot for her in his garage and let her stay the night. In the morning, his wife helped her become clean. She bandaged Habiba's feet, which had become cut and sore from all her walking. She gave her fresh clothes and shoes. Finally, she took her to a shelter run by a charitable organization.

This was the most kindness Habiba had been shown in so long. She was speechless with gratitude. Tears rolled down her face as she choked back sobs and went in to sign up for a bed.

Unfortunately, the shelter had a rule that a person could use a bed for only three days at a time. "There are so many people that need help in this city. We can only help so many at a time. I'm sorry." The young woman who told her this looked genuinely remorseful as she led the way to the outside through a rear exit. "You can come back in a month." This was more than anyone in her family had ever told her, even when they had shown her the door.

She had tried to adjust to living on the streets. She had tried to make friends with some of the people who were in similar situations to her own or people she recognized from the shelter. But most of these people scared her. They had been rejected by their families also, but some were clearly in need of mental health care or were recovering from problems that continued to plague them. They would never find the rest they needed. When one small group of people found out Habiba was sick, they became scared that they would catch what she had and threatened to attack her if she did not leave them alone. She tried to explain that she had internal problems and was recovering from cancer. They threw rocks at her and told her she was not welcome to return.

She would find food by scavenging sometimes, other times with donations from charitable organizations that handed out sandwiches. She considered herself especially lucky if she found out where this was taking place; these organizations never seemed to visit the same streets twice.

When she returned to the shelter, a counselor tried to help her by asking if she had any family or friends who might take her in. Habiba explained how she had run out of family and had nowhere else to turn. She told this overworked but kind young man about her health problems and how she was in constant pain. "It is a miracle you are alive," he told her. She knew he was right.

The next time she went to the shelter, it was already full. She went night after night but was too slow because of all the pain she felt and the damage that had been done to her feet. On the last night, she literally crawled there only to find a locked gate and a closed door. She crawled back to the nearest corner, drew her knees up to her chest, and stayed for as long as she was able.

This was her life now. Broken, hungry, starving, in pain, and with no one to help her and nowhere to go, Habiba struggled every day to stay alive and every night trying to sleep enough to gather up the strength to live. When the rainy season of autumn began, she wasn't sure whether to hope for the chance to live through it or to simply die of pneumonia and be done with everything.

She pressed her hands to the stone of the building as if clinging to the face of a cliff. She thought about all she had suffered but knew she wanted to continue living. She wanted to see her son again. She wanted to make peace with how she had lived her life. She did not want it to end this way.

Habiba shivered with cold, but her face felt warm with hope. But at that moment, another spasm of pain shot through her whole body. She could not stand through it and collapsed to the ground. She thought she could silently endure it, as she had so much, but the pain intensified. Habiba screamed.

Through the haze of her anguish, she saw two women approach her. She feared they would try to eject her or beat her since she was so helpless. Habiba tried to raise her hands to defend herself but lacked the strength to move.

The women stood over her. She could see they were young but could not hear what they were saying. Their eyes were full of pity and concern, but Habiba was still scared. The young women bent down and picked her up. They carried her off, but she did not know where. Confused and scared but still holding on to hope, Habiba passed out.

Chapter 12

2003

"Happy birthday!"

Everyone sang the traditional song. It was painfully out of tune, but Habiba thought it was the most beautiful melody she had ever heard in her life. It reminded her of songs she'd heard at weddings, which always made her happy despite what they had meant to her in the past. She was always able to preserve that initial happiness, and no one and nothing had managed to take that away from her.

There were communal dishes full of food set out, with a traditional Moroccan chocolate cake in the center. It was basically a large chocolate tea cake topped with fresh fruit, but none of the guests could wait to try it. It had even been made according to Habiba's dietary restrictions! Birthdays were not a common celebration in Morocco, even in Casablanca, but Habiba was turning fifty today and all of her new friends wanted to show her how thankful they were that she was alive.

They were lower-class people, nothing at all like her family or her former husband. Her friends were janitors, clerks, counselors, case workers. Many were former addicts or convicts. Most of her female friends had also left abusive husbands; some of them had been rejected by their families for doing so, told they had to stay in such situations no matter what because a woman's place was with her husband.

They had careers but lived modestly. They lived simple lives but got along. There were only about six people in Habiba's home, and the food spread out was a bit meager and conventional. But everyone was having a good time and no one was going without food. Her house was small, but it suited her. It was quaint, clean, cozy, and certainly better than the street or a cot in a spare room. It had a bedroom, a living room, a bathroom. What more could she possibly need?
This was certainly the best birthday she had ever celebrated. More than that, she considered it the happiest day of her life.

After cake had been served and everyone stood around talking, Habiba gathered up some of the dishes and took them into her kitchen to at least soak them. She didn't want to let them pile up during the party and end up with too much work at the end of the night. As the sink filled with water, she thought back to that rainy night that had changed everything.

* * *

They had taken her to a women's shelter, but Habiba did not realize that until much later. She had woken up in a hospital bed with an IV in her arm. She didn't know what was happening and was confused but no longer scared. Whoever had taken her was clearly trying to help her. She was a bit groggy but could feel bandages on her feet and head. She didn't even know she'd had a head wound. She drifted back into unconsciousness, much less worried than she'd been when she woke up.

When she woke up again, she could see the pink light of sunset streaming through a window at the other end of the room. There were six other beds, all of them occupied. Everyone was sleeping soundly and comfortably. She didn't want to wake anyone but wanted to find out where she was. "Hello," said a man's voice, soft and gentle. He approached the foot of her bed and waved politely. He had the kindest eyes she had ever seen.

He explained to Habiba that she was in a shelter for women and was welcome to stay as long as she was able. She would receive medical care, food, and clothing. This was her bed, and she would speak to doctors and counselors in the morning. "For now, you just continue to get your rest. Have sweet dreams and know that your worries are over," he finished.

Habiba stayed there for almost a year. She consulted with several doctors, who all marveled at how she had survived. More than one commented on how she was in much better shape than they expected, given what she had been through. There was no trace of cancer or kidney disease; most of her ailments had been the result of malnutrition. She attended group therapy sessions for people who had been through trauma and made many friends, learning the true definition of family.

When she was ready to leave, the agency that ran the shelter helped her move in to her house. They provided her with sheets for her bed, clothes for her back, and plates and cups for her cupboard. There was nothing extravagant, but it was more than enough for her to live, and live happily. She never saw the young women who had initially carried her off the street, never learned their names. A part of Habiba could not help but wonder if they'd been angels.

* * *

Habiba turned off the water and let the dishes soak. She decided to get back to her guests. It was her party, after all, and she did not want anyone to feel neglected. She was happy that so many people had been able to make it. Tears welled up in her eyes, but she blinked them away. Instead, she let out a long, contented sigh. After so much pain and neglect, she was where she had always longed to be, surrounded by love. She was at peace with her life.

Seeing her from the kitchen, standing at the edge of the room, one of her friends held up his glass and offered a toast. "To lovely Habiba!" Everyone raised a glass to her.

Chapter 13

2004

Habiba had been in her house for a year now and her life had settled into a comfortable rhythm. She earned a little money performing odd jobs for people around her neighborhood and met with her friends regularly for tea. She would read books at night before bed. The women's center that had so transformed her life asked her to speak to a few of the women they had recently rescued to help them cultivate their newfound hope for life. She wanted for nothing and may have felt guilty asking for anything more than what she had been given.

However happy she was, though, she sometimes thought of her son. Did Mohammed ever think about her? Did he try to find her after they had lost touch so long ago? How was he living? She hoped he was happy. She sometimes thought about trying to find him but did not know where to begin to look. The people at the shelter may have known people, but she did not want to ask them. They had given her so much already.

Whenever thoughts of Mohammed strayed into her mind, Habiba reminded herself that she was happy enough. It saddened her that she did not know what was happening in his life, but she quietly accepted the idea that she may never see him again or learn what had happened to him and Latifa. She had everything she would ever need and wanted nothing more.

One morning, there was a knock on her door. At first, she

thought it was nothing. She wasn't expecting anyone. There was another knock. She did not know who it could be but went to the door. "Hold on, please," she called out. "I'm coming!" Her health was greatly improved, but she still walked slowly for a woman her age. These aches and pains would be with her the rest of her life.

When she opened the door, she saw a middle-aged man staring back at her. His shoulders were slumped, his head bowed, and he held his hands in front of him. He appeared nervous and chastened. She recognized him instantly. "My son!" she cried with more joy than someone would have thought possible for such a small woman.

"Mother," Mohammed said. Before he could utter another word, though, she had thrown her arms around his neck. She kissed his cheek and pressed her face against his. He weeped in turn, overwhelmed at how happy she was to see him. "Forgive me," he whispered.

She looked into his eyes without letting him go and said, "There is nothing to forgive."

When they had finally composed themselves, he had some bad news. "Mother," he told her, "I have lost my job. They have taken my house and I have had to sell most of my possessions. Is it possible . . . Could I . . . May Latifa and I . . ."

Habiba put her hand on her son's shoulder. "You have always been welcome here."

Mohammed could not find the words to thank her. He gave her a big hug and told her he would be right back. She did not move from her front step until he returned, nor did she stop smiling in anticipation the entire time.

The sight that greeted her pleased her even more than the reunion with her son. Mohammed had a small boy in his arms and was holding the hand of a little girl. They both took after him, though they had the fairer hair of their mother. Latifa was walking behind them. She had gained a bit of weight over the years, but it suited her. There was a maturity in her bearing that had been lacking when she married Mohammed. She still held her head high, but there was a humility that gave her a more authoritative bearing.

"I would like you to meet Said," Mohammed said, offering the boy up to Habiba's arms. She took him gladly. "He is six years old and has already started school." He presented the little girl holding his hand. "And this is Habiba." He looked into his mother's eyes and smiled. "She is eight years old and very wise and beautiful."

Habiba could hardly contain herself. "It is so wonderful to meet such bright and happy little ones!"

Mohammed beamed with pride. "Children, this is your grandmother."

* * *

There wasn't much room, but they made it work. Mohammed and Latifa refused to take the bed, even though Habiba offered it to them. Instead, her grandchildren slept with her, surrounded by comfortable pillows.

Latifa had indeed grown a great deal as a wife, mother, and woman. She treated her mother-in-law with nothing but respect and deference. "I'm sorry I did not find a way for you to live with us," she said. She worked hard to make up for her past shortcomings, doing most of the housework and all the shopping. When the children were at school, she would not let Habiba lift a finger. The two women spent their days catching up and living like old friends.

Habiba felt whole now. Her life was complete and perfect.

All that she had lost had been returned, and more. Her son had come back to her—with grandchildren! She was a woman defined by joy. She was truly blessed beyond her deepest imagining.

Chapter 14

2005

It was the end. Everyone knew it, but no one wanted to say it. Habiba had held on for so long, but there was nothing anyone could do. Mohammed had brought in several doctors to help her. She had been to the hospital several times. She was only fifty-two years old but had lived through several lifetimes. Her body had simply reached its limit. Now everyone stood vigilant to say good-bye.

They were in Mohammed's new house. He had gotten a new job only a few months after moving in with Habiba, and they were able to afford something much larger. The children each had their own rooms. Habiba had been given a number of rooms so that she could do whatever she wished. She spent her last few days in total comfort. Said and Habiba had grown to love their grandmother so much. They had spent every spare second with her, and they all showered affection on each other with such abundance.

Her friends had all come to visit. They came every night, whenever any of them were free. No matter how far they had to travel or what other obligations they may have had, they wanted to also pay their respects to Habiba and say good-bye properly. She had made their lives better in the short time she had been in them.

Latifa was pregnant again. She had only recently begun to

show, but she and Mohammed had insisted that Habiba would be around to see this baby born. She knew better. Now, lying in bed, barely able to speak or move, she motioned Latifa to come to her. Latifa walked over slowly and bent her head low toward Habiba so she could hear what she had to say.

"You are a good mother. Your children will be happy. Thank you for making my grandchildren happy."

The children could not stop crying, but they were quiet now. They had run out of breath and strength to continue as they had been.

Habiba thought back on the last forty years of her life. She had struggled more than she would have expected. She had endured more pain than many people had thought possible, especially for one woman alone in the world. In the end, she had one year of perfect happiness. She was glad for that. She thought of how she must look now, her eyes starting to glaze above sunken cheeks. Her hair was thin and she had lost teeth. Her name meant *lovely*. "I'm not as beautiful as I used to be," she said with a hoarse laugh.

Mohammed sat down next to her and took her hands in his. "You are my mother," he said. "You are Habiba. You are lovely." He let his tears flow freely and squeezed her hands.

Her lips formed a cracked, imperfect smile that made everyone happy. She tried to say thank you but lacked the strength. Habiba's eyes were suddenly full of light. She breathed her last breath and passed away.

www.ingramcontent.com/pod-product-compliance
Lightning Source LLC
Chambersburg PA
CBHW070101100426
42743CB00012B/2628